Clemency

BOOKS BY COLETTE INEZ

The Woman Who Loved Worms
Alive and Taking Names
Eight Minutes from the Sun
Family Life
Getting Under Way: New & Selected Poetry
Naming the Moons
For Reasons of Music
Clemency

Clemency

poems by
Colette Inez

A Brenadine C. Humphrey Selection

Carnegie Mellon University Press
Pittsburgh 1998

ACKNOWLEDGMENTS

I would like to thank Charlotte Mandel, Pamela "Jody" Stewart and Wendy Ranan for invaluable suggestions in perfecting a number of these poems. I am also indebted to Robert Schultz who encouraged me to write this book. A 1995 fellowship from The New York Foundation for the Arts afforded me cherished time to work on the manuscript, as did residencies at Yaddo, the MacDowell Colony, Blue Mountain Center, Ucross Foundation and the Virginia Center for the Creative Arts. My gratitude also extends to Bucknell University for my post as poet-in-residence at The Stadler Center for Poetry.

Poems in this collection originally appeared, some in slightly different form, in these publications whose editors I would like to thank: *Denver Quarterly*, "Refrain for My Sires," "In My Cousin's Apartment, Paris 1994, Two Years After My Mother's Death," "Maunderings at Lammastide"; *Sycamore Review*, "A Story"; *Antioch Review*, "I Describe My Parents Before They Know They Have Made Me Come True," "Marthe's Almanac"; *New England Review*, "The Play of Lovers," "The Music Box," "My Priest Father's Words," "Clemency" (originally titled "I Clasp Another's Hands as if She Were My Child"); *New York Quarterly*, "How Did They Recognize Autumn in the Dark of the City?," "Journeys," "The Perseid Meteors of August"; *Hudson Review*, "The Telling," "Oxford Meeting"; *Crosscurrents*, "Hybrid Song"; *Northwest Review*, "Orphanage Sisters"; *Poetry Now*, "Monday's Children"; *Cimarron Review*,"Found Child"; *Ohio Review*, "Confounded Song","My Mother's Counsels", "Mirror Story"; *Lullwater Review*, "Royal Coach Taking the Queen"; *Canto*, "It Didn't Serve Us Right"; *Raccoon*, "Old Woman Out of Iowa", "My Father In A Garden"; *New Letters*, "Dee's Migraines", "The Return"; *West Branch*, "Waves at Lakeside", "Teaching Junior High at Castle Hill"; *Bennington Review*, "In Every Sense Corrective Ink Is Running Out"; *Poetry Review*, "Word Circuits, Solitary"; *Chariton Review*, "Ghazals for October"; *Seattle Review*, "Mother Song"; *Parnassus: Poetry in Review*, "Lady in the Stacks"; *Wittenberg Review*, "Thinking of My Parisian Mother's Discretion . . ."; *Quarter Past Eight*, "The House of Dreams", "My Father and the Lord of Null"; *Helicon Nine*, "Second Visit", "Writing Letters to My Mother", "Reveries While Landing on the Coast"; *The American Voice*, "Day Visitor, Susquehanna University"; *Colorado Review*, "Dream Shore", "August Atoms"; *Iowa Review*, "The Wig of Liliane"; *Massachusetts Review*, "Things Dream of Their Likenesses and Needs", "Encounter at the Jardins Botaniques"; *Indiana Review*, "Moth Dream of My Late Therapist"; *Folio*, "In Praise of Outlines"; *Sycamore Review*, "In a Garen"; *New York Poetry*, "Consolation of Blood and Irises"; *The Bitter Oleander*, "Fire in the Prairie"; *Connecticut Review*, "Valéry Joins Me and My Newfound Cousⁱ in Nérac"; *Black Moon*, "Blood Relations".

TABLE OF CONTENTS

III

For Saul
with love and gratitude

I

REFRAIN FOR MY SIRES

Intertwined ironweed and wild roses
where the snake raced away
from whispering creatures in the grass,

two who presumed God fused the hour
of sparrows to St. Francis's morsels of bread,
not that I would be born out of their bodies.

He sleeps under the shadow of a mountain,
she in a great iron bed, his blessings
in her dream of kneeling in the grass.

Water, Mary Mother blue. Ashes of rose.
Fish doze in deep pools, baptismal silver.
I, born from these lovers' bodies,

would swim out of their spasms and cries.
I can never tell them, embraced in their gaze,
I too have wept in dry grass

beneath stars like rue anemones in the open woods,
I, who was born from these lovers' bodies,
closed eyes, tongue numb, their flesh in the grass.

A STORY

There were rumors of a priest old enough
to be her father. She was the Latinist
he needed for his work on medieval texts.
Her family had no reason to suspect

her deference to a learned man.
She wrote she was swayed by his fame
as an Aristotle scholar
after I asked had she ever loved him.

When her clothes strained at the seams,
both may have talked of crossing
the border into Belgium.
I don't know. No one must know,

they agreed, except their confessor,
and a colleague or two.
Dust on cathedral windows,
gathered in bouquets,

shook out again in wind and rain.
Birds migrated, wedge shaped shadows
on deltas and plateaus.
In the sacristy, among surplices and robes,

he paced, a man clouded over with regret
for the child he might not hold.
And the woman lodged in another country?
My father did not hear her screams

pierce the leaves as I unfurled.
Clouds like bridal veils drifted above the city.
Hidden with the Sisters in an outlying part,
I grew where flowers took root in dry fields.

Soon the priest will be buried near the sea,
but my mother would grow old, recording parchments
and tomes on the history of the church.
After she slides into earth, nothing

of his name, nor mine, not a scrap
will be found in locked boxes or her vaults.
None will guess a child had slipped out
of those delicate thighs. And I will have my say.

I Describe My Parents Before They Know They Have Made Me Come True

In the cloister of Saint Odilo
fountain water speaks in a language
of brief syllables.
Gray light mottles terra-cotta.

A woman enters the courtyard.
Nothing stirs but the flutter of leaves.
In step beside her, a husky man
in a clerical collar carries

papers and books.
He gazes at her somber face.
Soon birds fly out of the jade plant,
peck at his clenched hands,

pull at her damp hair. Draw blood.
Together they cry like a wind
through fronds. A mistral.
They do not know I am with them.

He murmurs in his lover's ear
soon he will break
with the Order.
Again she unknots

the intricate ties of her robe,
kisses the welts
where his collar cut.
Her moans are woven of fur and bone.

Like a blind cave fish
I brush against the shell of her trance.
This pair does not know I will be born.
Nothing I do will change them.

THE PLAY OF LOVERS

Pears soft to the thumb, wine.
Now the sun is the moon, each
look a new word, phrases to arrange
like roses in a vase.

Lovers. Everyone has seen them fall
into a blur of change; one leaf
and then another on the lawn. Shade
gives way to light. Snow comes down.
Do you see them, two figures
in the distance making their small mark?

Words too submit to years. Plain
flowers in the yard repeat their trick
of vanishing. The sun is the sun
and each look is seen again and again
until the faces disappear.
Everyone has seen it.

How Did They Recognize Autumn in the Dark of the City?

A crucifix over the bed,
a tremor of shadows and the moon
flying low like an owl into their room
gave no hint I might arrive, purple and curled,
a child begun in a reverie

of autumn. Like a rain cloud he burst
into the dream from which she woke to Burgundy
masked by peppermint, silver bristles
of his chin rubbing her cheek, neck.
Inhaling her scents, lavender and library paste,
he barely guessed she longed to straggle after birds

over the Seine, away from the biblioteque that penned her
in rooms whose knowledge he desired as he longed for her
flesh to tremble beneath him. She did not confess
to doubts of ministering to his needs.
When she wept, he kissed her flight
of tears, pressed his hand to her lips, gesturing

their secret. Summer had vanished like a wafer
on the tongue at Mass. Both knew time by chrysanthemum
stars blowing quills of light on the city,
from the wind's rasp and pulp of leaves,
by the stir of a child they would barely know,

one who would celebrate the union of heaven and earth,
and their coupling in the shadow of Notre Dame
whose gargoyle gabbled waters sounded waves
of applause resonating in an autumn squall.

THE TELLING

They sit in the refectory
by the closed kitchen door.
October rain blurs the tall windows.
They have met here before to part with secrets.

Morning light brushes gray on bare walls,
fingers his carrot colored hair.
A wedge of lines deepens between her gold eyes.
She peers at the swelling

under her coat, forms a steeple with her hands,
daydreams holy water blessing the baby's face,
a saint's name for the christening.
He tugs at his collar and blinks.

Pots and pans clattering in the kitchen tell them
they're no longer alone.
Her fingers tense as he skims them with his lips.
They leave by different doors.

Inside her body, a fury of division seizes
attributes from each: yellow-brown eyes,
a fringe of auburn curls
bloom into the parcel delivered to the Sisters.

Late June — a whiff of incense and convent roses
in my bassinet.

Hybrid Song

Child of mother fish,
child of father oak,
when you arrived half gills,
half leaves

you were pushed off to swim
in a far off glade.
With fins to let your life glide on,
you trailed your roots

and told a lily in the snow
night and day rise equally,
that odd is beautiful.

Oak and fish denied
they mated in the rain.
Father fell on his knees
in a gale.

Mother swallowed another day.
You dawdled for years.
One day you found a grove of birds.
Who will love you? they cawed.

Birds at odds, you said.
When you found clouds,
who will you love? they sighed
from their long, white ships.

Preparing to stand your ground,
preparing to swim out far,
you were what you were.
Clouds, clouds, you answered them.

ORPHANAGE SISTERS

Uniform skills, blindstitch
for sale, we hemmed
for God's plan
in Africa, embroidered

dreams of pink and orange
countries on a map, 7 madonna
blue seas. That world on a scroll
pulled up and down.

Set over the blankets,
at night our hands
were peninsulas of flesh.
It was the rule of nuns and trustees

who came to spread the law
like disinfectant on the walls.
My sisters, I remember your braids
like sailors' ropes

when we sailed to Mass,
the confessionals of winter
swept away in the spring
of the war.

Continental drifts, Africa
bulges on a map.
I dream you loosen your hair
at the edge of great tides

in Antwerp and Ostend
where polders are green
as the palm trees of Jerusalem
we cross stitched for Christ.

MONDAY'S CHILDREN

So Tuesday, Shrove, Wednesday, Ash,
Maundy Thursday, Friday, Christ
propped on the wall
while we stripped for Saturday's bath,
six bowls of gruel and Sunday again.

We dreamt of booths and carnival priests.
Mary Virgin guessed our weight.
The barker spieled we will conceive
with no man's thing.
Pitched into dawn our nightgames ceased.

Freak tricks, the stars, the moon.
Kneel, sit, hulking nuns made us heel,
toe the mark, keep straight lines.
We thought the world flat, an orphanage floor.
Crossworlds of the gazetteer far beyond
our plaster saints.

So Monday, spuds, Tuesday, chard, mutton,
Thursday, Friday, fish slapped on a plate
while we swam in Saturday's bath,
six dreams of oceans and Sunday again.

Friday at the Institute

Under the figure of Our Lady
in the lopsided O of the moon,
I turn in an L-shaped ward.
Near me a boy dragged from sleep
spits out a dream
of a great trench.
Red leaves. Bloody snot.
Piss. A kick in the rump.

We queue up to the sink,
give our teeth a slap
of cold water, brush them with salt.
I name each tooth after a letter
tacked to the schoolroom wall,
the A-my-loose-molar,
B-abscessed...alphabets rehearsed
in pliant books marked by nuns.

At midday after the blessing
we spit fish bones on white plates,
wipe our lips with the backs
of our palms. We say the tables
up to twelve times twelve,
say it again,
file in line to pray.
Legs apart like the lower half of "X",
or an open ladder, the ashen faced

priest makes the sign. Allelujah,
that boy with spooky dreams and I
rub our eyes with smudged hands,
pick bits of mackerel from back teeth,
our fingernails rosy as Mary's teats
suckling the Blesséd Child.

LAST TROLLEY STOP, BRUSSELS

Not to twist the knob,
not to stumble past iron beds,
above each one, a crucifix.
Not to slide into the morning
half awake, shaken by bells in the tower.

I can almost see the blowy green
of courtyard trees,
almost hear the Sunday trolleys
that clattered us away
to Saint Julian's
haze of incense and Latin.

The war arrives, breaks us apart.
Three blasts of a ship's horn
and I salute another continent.

Not to open those soft books
in my first tongue.
My Belgium collects
muted blues and grays,
withdrawn days of snow blown shores.

Never to find my father
leaning against the rail
of a ship, his arm slung
about my shoulder, not
to think our kisses wake my mother
from her trance. Not

to have pressed her limp hands
to my face.

Pages turn the stories I invent.
I need to recall a tangerine red dress
and sailor-blue coat, the sky over Brussels
thrumming news of my trip.

A nun's cross clung to my damp chest
when I sailed. Fish faced devils heckled
and gibed from the bottom of the waves.

Now after a long fever, I turn
towards my husband.
We will catch the next boat, I say.
On my childhood street furrows of grass
camouflage the trolley tracks.

FOUND CHILD

My face as a child floats up
from a porcelain basin,
blue fleur-de-lis curled at the border,
and settles over mine like snow on a pond.

In the mirror I nod to the girl I was
kneeling at a prie-dieu.
She dug bare knees into wood, pressed her face
in her hands when she prayed

and would faint from too much fasting.
That I could turn a cold shoulder to the faith.
"Imbecile," she stamps her foot.
I tell her I want what I have:

love, books, scented candles, linen.
Even now she wants to allot these things to the poor
of the missions. When I hang back, she sobs,
wiping her nose on a square of rough cloth.

As I slip out of her face,
place it on a flowered pillow
moonlight smooths like a doting mother,
even now she tugs at my sleeve.

MIRROR STORY

The girl in the white pullover
and pale half slip falls mute,
bruised cheek in the mirror,
cut lip pressed in a kiss
she will blot out of memory.

Snow falls past the window.
A man's hand leaves marks on her.
Glass shattered from another quarrel
can't return her face to whole.
She looks ahead and runs
into the body of what took place.

Now if she were to step out of the glass,
I would cup that girl's face in my hands,
say to her look at me, look at me,
I have found a way to tell the story.
She would not know who I am.

JOURNEYS

Once my mother came by train
to a south shore town.
She made the sign of the cross
when she gave me away.

All aboard for
Valley Stream, Lynbrook,
Rockville Center, Baldwin,
Freeport, Merrick...
conductors call out in a litany.

Have your ticket ready,
all out for
Bellmore, Wantagh, Seaford,
Massapequa, Massapequa Park...

Sprinklers. Portable pools.
Clutching a toy boat,
a toddler flops in the water,
calls ma to the giant woman
who has gone indoors in
Amityville, Copague,
Lindenhurst, Babylon, Bay Shore...

My child floats where train
lines end, lives in towns
of my imaginings
where my mother claims me,
loves me like her rosary.

Royal Coaches Taking the Queen

That old woman negotiating the street
with two English canes shouted
Frenchie babu, stop,
you go on, you go on
but I loved how my words
rolled off at the edge
of dusty blue lines.
They were coaches for a queen
and her retinue to ride.
The air grows cold
with my summoning —
Nana's shoulder pokes out
of a mud colored coat,
her teeth don't fit.
Silence arrives in every size.
I rarely wore it. It didn't last,
not like her disdain
for me, hardbitten
and enduring even to the end
in the blaring white of the ward
where they rolled her away
like linen piled high
at the end of the week.
To her gray-brown wherever,
I send by coach and four
my ruby dress of consoling words.

BLOOD RELATIONS

In my red leatherette book of thoughts,
that girl you said was no blood relation
of yours, transformed you into a country dancer
your cheeks rouged with sliced beets,

cornstarch dabbed on your nose.
A beau raps at the farmhouse door, shifts
from foot to foot.
You slide a gloved hand over his arm.

The horse and buggy clip clops through snow.
Now a worn album of shots:
in a feathered hat, you are flanked
by steamer trunks.

Just married, you step away
from the church door, nose in the air.
Here you roll out pastry dough
next to a new gas range.

A wrecking ball swings at the house
where your first born ebbed away.
Grizzled, standing on two canes,
you pick out your tomb.

Grass parched where the coffin tilts . . .
"More scribbling," you'd whistled
through crinkled lips, eyes dulled over
when I enthused — I wanted to put the Luna moth green

cabbage, glistening in the sink, into a poem.
You clomped up the stairs
to face your partner's do-si-dos
in a dream of Iowa.

I praise your stubborn steps,
recast the questions
through which birds glide —
over the ashes of our calendars, my filled day books.

THE MUSIC BOX

A dancer spins
to a flickering tune:
My Bonnie Lies Over...
Nana lays her cane
on the lavender quilt
starts to brush her barbed white hair...
calls back the winter
she turned sixteen,
yellow hair swept up.
"Look," she spins around her mother
who dotes on memories of Glasgow
before she said aye to the Iowa
farmer. Staring out the window
into snow, "Leave me alone,"
says the mother —
the girl is waved away.

Slowly the music withdraws
from Nana's cramped room.
"Just leave me alone," her lips clench
when I offer a tumbler of water.
The long moan of no's.
O these solitary dancers,
now they lie under the wind that spins.
Nana has set down her dreams
to dance in a wooden box.
I twist the key and catch a shimmer
of what cannot be brought back.
Pinched with longing,
I dream I am rocked in a woman's arms.
My mother lies over the sea.

IT DIDN'T SERVE US RIGHT

"Pests," she griped when the crickets
sang. "Chamber music," I answered back.
"Serves them right," she used to gloat
at the carcasses of bugs stuck
to the screen. Massacres of summer,
moths, ants, fleas, ticks.

It didn't serve us right
to live in a greenhouse of ills.
I remember the last tremor
of her voice like a web-snared moth
at summer's end.

The racket of birds she didn't like
goes on at dusk, a raucous chorus
of cowbirds and grackles.
She has lain down now for forty years

in a quiet field. Alive, she was
mean. Dead, I hear her spirit
grand in the trees and rejoicing.

OLD WOMAN OUT OF IOWA

Insolent days of light and rain.
Sometimes she stared like someone who knew
the time had come to nothing, blamed me
for frazzling her nerves, cussed out her son, Ray,
for marrying so soon after Ruthie died of booze.

"Shut your mouth and stand up straight,"
she'd command. I slumped and called her witch
under my breath.
That summer didn't give a damn
about my pleas for calm.

I hunched over books, mystery, romance,
abandoned to mist and balustrades.
When Ray swung an axe at our door,
she stood on two canes,
ratty housecoat, gnarled hair.

I hid. The door caved in. She stared
him down. Later, he disappeared into
the junklot of drunken men.
Her hands were folded just so in the casket.
The summer wind combed back the leaves.

She was my witness, that woman out of Iowa.
She held her balance
on two canes and a midwestern will to stay
upright. Today, at her grave,
I throw my shoulders back in a grudging salute.

DEE'S MIGRAINES

How I envied the cherry wood
gleam of your thick pageboy,
its sweep at the shoulder,
oh ex-chorine, beauty pageant also-ran
with head splitting throbs in our ricky tick house.

You, who'd banged
my skull on the wall for using your cologne
and beat a retreat in a big shouldered
coat, brass studded belt, clanky jewels,
cocky in Tweed Lentherique, Tabu, hitting the bars
on Merrick Road. Do your migraines still blaze

or have they ebbed with memories of what's-her-name
who walked hunched up and chewed her nails?
I hold out my arms to that girl, but she skitters away
from your scowl in the mirror — you, sleek Dee,
slapping on war paint for an all night spree.

Sometimes late at night I collide into the girl's
fear, feel it quiver on tiptoe.
Your ice blue satin nightie's V
dives between U-shaped breasts.
Light from the bed hacks a path through smoke.
Pall Malls. One after another. Miltown and aspirin.

A migraine has settled in,
taut as your voice ordering a gin
straight up with a twist,
"and make it quick." I set up the drink and hum,
the migraine, my ally for hours to come.

WAVES AT LAKESIDE

The fly, the table,
the glass with ice
in it melting,
her manicured hands
on the glass
or shooing off the fly,
are poised at the edge
of a lake fanned by swallows
and dragonflies, stirred by fish.
The woman at the table
filters the afternoon
through different colors
from the fly's
shifts of ultraviolets
as it fights to crawl
out of the glass.
What do they see, the woman's
large eyes reflected
in the high gloss of the table,
in the half empty glass?
She flicks the drowned fly
to the grass,
dreams of breaking out
of the chronic winter white
to come, the lake caged in ice.

GRANDMOTHER AND CHILD ARE SET TO LISTEN ON SUNDAY NIGHTS

Her patchy white hair in a net,
the woman hushes the child whose shiny bob
is held by a barrette. They tip back
their heads as radio waves
bring them Mr. Anthony, advisor.
"Madame, no names or addresses, please."

Woeful stories dip
and skitter like swallows.
"My husband went out for a quart of Four Roses
and never came back. I have a question,"
somebody pleads between sobs.
"O Mr. Agony," the child revels
in the theater of faraway grief.

"Madame, try to control yourself,"
she mimics the counselor.
The grandmother glances at a picture of her son,
slick-haired in a suit and tie.
After a quart of Four Roses, he'd kick down the door.
A child's "no, no" in an upstairs room.
Static crackles in the woman's skull.

Iowa, winter. Her father's hands under the coverlet.
His moonshine breath, a ghost in the room.
"I'll tell the minister," she warned.
In a dream she asks a man she can't describe:
"Do you have an answer?"

THE RETURN

Purple voices bruised in rooms of booze —
mauling wartime tunes,
Coming in on a Wing . . .
jitterbug, jive and cutting a rug.

I have to haul that carpet away, the one
with the grape jelly stains I couldn't wipe out
though I scrubbed on my knees like a postulant
entreating Saint Jude not to be slapped.

I have to rake away those wary hours,
pile them in a bin, invoke St. Ursula
for their credible death.
...Cliffs of Dover...Don't Sit Under...

The Andrews Sisters, Catholic Sisters
on a conga line of recall.
Caissons keep rolling.
Dazed soldiers, the years stand guard

posted to distant wars. Like a ball of foil
the sun glitters down on me. I'm coming back
to sky write: CEASE FIRE,
to crowd the house with doves.

II

OXFORD MEETING

Lodging house,
fringed lamps
in the foyer.
I say who I am.
She motions me upstairs.
Rumpled hose, elbows
poking through holes
of a potato colored
cardigan, astonishment
drawn in lines
at her mouth.
Curved like mine
her hips shift weight
on an opposite chair.
She asks what I want.
I look for a sign
she has looked for me —
letters returned
addressee unknown.
A photograph.
The wall clock
hatches an hour.
Streaked white mane,
disheveled at the neck,
this woman
was the furtive girl
fingering her rosary,
buttons strained
when she took
the train north
to place me in a cradle
strangers might rock.
Now she communes
with a spirit
just past my gaze.
"You may write to me,

not saying who we are."
She sees me to the door.
Pallid roses of snow
fall as I leave.
I hunger for the color
of fire, orange balloons
floating through ashes.

In Every Sense Corrective
Ink Is Running Out

Bull headed? I suppose I was blunt
where I should have been fine edged.
Sometimes I got in the way like the cat
at our icebox door when my uncle Ed
loved corn: fritters, soup, niblets, flakes.

Set against the summer we grew into uniforms
the times had ironed smooth, ovals for me
a broken line for him.
The slate received our effigies in chalk,
the landslide of his throat, my uneventfulness.

There were others in the frame, secondary
characters, a well mannered boy favors
me in green. He disappears one afternoon.
Flawed episodes, invented tones.
A secret mother who'd waived her rights

to count the buttons of my coat. Rich woman.
Poor woman. Paris, November, stations of rain.
Love's injunction to stay turbulent. Barcelona.
Toulouse. I convalesce.

The mystery of good naturedness.
Will I pull myself up with proverbial lines?
I travel to the Continent
looking for my mother in sleepytime Britain
after the war. Genetrix, she takes the measure

of my voice. A moment's glance reveals
I don't resemble her family branch.
My digestion is poor, she tells me in a look.
I go away.

The corrective ink is running out, errors
refuse to give way. I was a mistake but hold on
to my place. "You can't imagine," she started
to say and yes, how could I have prayed in her
chapel of regrets? I was the gist of our story.

Page of the House of Trees,
the early ruckus of the world is in us.
My mother's text. Patron Saint of Blue,
I write it down to set it straight,
to redeem my life.

WORD CIRCUITS, SOLITARY

When I looked at her, I had French sounds
my lips pushed into air.
"*Je suis ta fille.*" Pronoun, verb, pronoun,
noun, all in proper order. Not "I your daughter am."
My mother gripped the banister.

It was her habit to correct my letters,
crossing out errors in red ink. My French
on the page bled from its wounds but stumbled on
like a courier carrying a message that refused
to be lost. Lost and found.

When I found a word I'd lost I'd pounce on it
as if it were a purse returned or a prodigal friend
standing in the doorway of my house. Outside, the sky
would boast the usual array of periods and asterisks,
a delicate script studied in towers and ships.

I used words, therefore I was, wasn't I? When I wed
the man framed against the sky, we said what my parents
never said, "I do" in a ritual sense. After the annulment,
I battered that man with chattering. He bruised me
with blows of silent days. Him. Them. My mother,

her mother, hers. Everything they said
about birth is dead or waits to be reborn.
Why do I muse on the question: is death a shift
of chemicals? Look for my atoms in a school of fish,
a distant snow, a nebula's veil in a diffuse dream

in the marriage of great galaxies. Language, a stay
against death. And I? Will I die
with a wreath of speech hung in a chapel for the bereaved,
clichés of lament arranged in a spray, a corsage
of nimble phrases pinned to my shroud?

In the afterworld, I imagine stuttering something
or other to myself and ghosts afflicted with sentences.
One of them might say: the water staggers
to the shore, absolves the rain of flooded towns.
Another: twirling its yellow knob,
the moon lets out a rush of hours, making a path
in the known circuits of the universe.

GHAZALS FOR OCTOBER

I

Moongauze of white lunar moth,
let me consult a shaman.

My powers unused, a kind of pain in the middle
of a diamond afternoon. Where's the old hoopla?

There must be a place for the merely willing.
Backpackers and boneheads hacking worn trails.

Moon's continuum. I go on,
part of me fading like a bolt of wool.

There's a zipcode of stone I'm being mailed to.
Dead letters of my name.

II

Homage to my mother.
Moonflakes of dusty moth.

She has the habit of leaves and remembers their lobes
in the private reprieve of her forest.

Frogs and grubs sing green. Larval masks. The praying mantiscocks
its head like an existential mandarin.

Concoction of clouds. An interplay of highborn words:
cathedral, decorum.

What is empty dies out from not being filled.
The hive exhales the swarm, the dusty pollen of the sun.

III

Put my father's cassock in a frame.
It cannot strut from habit and conceit.

Who consults with calendars deals in charades.
It was always this time in the silence of grief.

Lascivious ferns beyond the city's frame, leaves erect.
All mating takes place in an intricate hive.

Go and ask toads about the moon. Masked tribes
mumble in a trail of chards.

One season glides, another turns slowly on a spit.
We couple for continuum.

IV

The Philippine headache cure. My ache is that ball
the dung beetle moves uphill like Sisyphus.

I name the color of my pain. Brown. Here gleams my chalice,
the cup of my mother's monthly blood.

Conception in a secret cupboard. Let the sepia
pour into this flask.

Some things are doomed to moving dung.
I'm ready to speak of nostrums and cures.

The trail of the Philippine shaman
is heaped with green and intricate ills.

MOTHER SONG

Why did I picture a crucifix revolving
in your brain, and a flickering of gloss and text
so fine, my eyes felt like dull instruments?
You, who shuttled from archives to Mass
and back, papers in your arms, folios and notes.
Narrow steps in lecture halls and church,
you, who kept time to a music I neither read nor scored.

The music you did not hear flows in quiet bands.
My *Sur le Pont* . . . my *Cadet Rouselle*, the words
I used to explain occurrences, random and planned.
Words once spoken die. When I was a child, each day
I saw them plunge receding into emptiness.
The music I did not hear rippled from your house.
Your Chopin and Chaminade coaxed from the piano.

Childhood duets and caroling, the fray of talk
you fled from, solaced by books.
I see your alphabet in an abattoir —
letters splattered on the wall. Or in the dust
of a gutted school, abc's dismantled
where nuns cracked palms with the flat end
of a stick? Do words burn? Our papers will breed
a mountain of ashes, our commas, minuscule words

to devour almanacs of sentences.
Your voice played the keyboard of nouns
and verbs, a harmony of paragraphs. High and cool
in a muffling snow, winters ago. Whatever you said
crouches low in a node of memory.
That cold hour's sound, the whistle and sigh of the wind.
Sometimes, I wanted to be lost in your syllables,

to hear them leap like skiers from frozen slopes,
words thawed, tumbling in a stream of speech.
I am resigned to my fall from grace.
Christ's letter in a ghostly script
is not addressed to me.
Grace commencing with G, fifth tone in the modal major
scale, dives from the back of the throat,

swansong of g, gone, ground down by use.
One day, by electromechanical means,
science may extract words of talk held years before,
rescue what you said when we met after mute years,
my words as petitioners,
the noise love made when I curved my tongue,
words implanted in molecules,

locked in vibrating hearts.
Once I was your other heart, a double
tapping in your body when you tuned to the music
of my birth and we spoke without words.

MY MOTHER AND CARTOGRAPHY

I scan your face as if it were the map of France,
a five pointed star. Do I resemble you
in the foothills of the Pyrenees, in Tarbes, Lourdes, Pau?
Does your northern point in Dunquerque hug the Belgian
border where you hauled me into birth? A forehead's
width, do we share that? Not your hairline in Brittany
and Alsace, cheekbones in Poitou and Chalon, sly mouth
pursed in Aubusson. If I were to give my face to you
as a replica of France, would I have to explain:
here is my highest, lowest point, seasonal lakes, salt
flats, cascades. Would you then be moved to look at me,
to speak my name here in your mother country?

I study your body as if it were the map of France,
and I, a cartographer learning your conversion scales,
permanent streams, principle rivers and roads. Where
do I favor you most? It's idle to deny your collar bone
in Picardie and the likeness of our throats.
Is it possible in Creuse or Allier I inhabited
your womb for the customary term, that our internal
boundaries were the same? Did you wonder, a daughter or
son when I howled into the June air of Brabant,
north of a lowland country?

But you are not in France nor am I your cartographer.
I never read your legs in Gascony and Dauphin, and
when we met north of Touquet that first time, I didn't
measure your crosshatched lines, brackets poised
along your mouth, the distance you held in miles.
When you walked away, your feet didn't wade in Vence and
Hendaye, never idly rocked at low tide along the docks
of Menton or St. Jean de Luz in the southwestern cusp
of France's star. Your body and face slowly made their way
from morning to morning in a cold country,
neither yours nor mine.

Years later, you won't read what I must write,
my system of location drawn on paper and in ink. You sit
and look at the gravel pit where vineyards once grew
to the river's edge. You, gone back to your place of birth,
to Nérac, a physical world defined, east of Gironde,
west of Cestas, you, my mountain, my capital, my star,
my scholar mother now circling words in your mother tongue.

Shall I offer you the map of my forbearance, hachures
and grids, time zones and rifts to be your keepsakes in
the thinning years? I will address this gift to you
in your river house, my high-minded lady of France, you
who now present me to your tenants as a friend
from America, a far and marvelous country.

LADY IN THE STACKS

I

You, in the dust of the Biblioteque
Nationale indexing the Popes, Leo Xs
in their capelets of fur, high-minded
Lady Em in your cloche, clodhoppers
and woolen hose cutting a figure
in the archives of lost saints.

My tracer of missing flagellants,
you fingered codicils in the Vatican.
Ladder rungs were scuffed with your climb
to beatitudes shelved in the dust
of Lourdes. You sought an account
from Bernadette who scrubbed

for Christ, our Lord, faith
in the perfect floor. Lady Em, you
to whom I was more than a footnote
on the page of a crosschecked gloss,
I hold the fading words of this worn
chronicle, my scholar, my lost mother.

II

Mama, a pen, mama, a page,
I never said to you.
This is a story, these are my dreams,
my name, you never said to me.
We wrote correct letters over years
and let books fade in the light
of our rooms.

You would not say who I was.
I told my story again and again
trying to get it clear.

III

Medievalist, my mother, I was your text.
Need I account for your absences or mine,
the omission of shoehorns and bells
in a mother-daughter chronicle
of commonplace ways?

In the shadow of the priest's robe,
confessional booth and penances,
I, a veiled figure in your dreams
of sackcloth and ashes.

You asked for my silence and I prayed;
"Mary, intercede on my mother's behalf,"
I, your daughter, upholder of words,
reconciled to your diffidence.

THINKING OF MY PARISIAN MOTHER'S
DISCRETION (ONLY HER CONFESSOR KNOWS)
IN NOT TELLING HER SISTER
OR HARDLY ANYONE ABOUT MY BIRTH

Don't nobody know about us, Mama,
excepting everybody in central Ohio
and south. Even your plain French
name is anagrammed in print and
your letters quoted from.

Daddy's work for God has been told
straight out in Gambier, Granville,
Westerville to the folks who listen
in the audience. I've gone on to

explain he was a man of the cloth
and paid to keep a confidence.
Shooting off my mouth? Poetry's how
I keep my time from splintering

apart. Secrets, Mama. What's the point?
As long as you don't know I've made you
into literature and Daddy into a man
who fusses on stage, unsnaps his collar,
lets fall his robe beside the bed where

a woman lies down. That's you, Mama,
ready to enjoy yourself. The play's set
in the Fall and I watch its pages turn
in a long run of words I try to rake
into piles for burning.

I don't want to be buried in church lore
or dead to the child who poked
out its head between my legs.
Shoot, Mama, is that too
much to understand? They all cheered me
in Cincinnati and Steubenville.

THE HOUSE OF DREAMS

My mother's house beckons me to the other side of the bridge crossing the Garonne. Why am I hunting for photographs that don't exist? My mother and father as two-backed beasts or a gentle pair picking cinquefoil in the woods, a picture of me and my mother in my arms or I in hers. We can be old and love cream colored roses of reflected light fading from view. We can sit by the river and remember my father's sermons on humility. Is that it? No, a thin cloth of moon dabs at the dark as if it were a wound. This isn't the journey I want. The photographs sleep at the bottom of a box in my mother's house of dreams.

SECOND VISIT

In a French castle town I hurry
to my mother's house.
Ducks exult, geese chant
over the river in a clatter of rain.
Diminutive queen of fox gloves and lilies,
she beckons me inside.
I have not seen her in thirty years;
her white hair falls in wisps
around her somber face.
"My American friend," she presents me
to her tenants. They nod and disappear.
When I smile, does she recall
my father's lips skimming her throat,
narrow shoulders and breasts, full as mine
under my sweater? Our talk is thin.
I slump in a chair.
How easy to slip into her design
for making me invisible.
In this book of moments she remains
my hesitant guide to the marvels
of her country. I did not wish for
your birth, she once wrote, my lady
of steadfast penmanship, paramour
to the reverend who begot me in a dream.
These two who hunched over Ovid's
Art of Love and Juvenal's *The Vanity
of Human Wishes* in my fantasy of them,
also scanned October's book of leaves
when I was conceived.
No need to say I was resolved to be born
in a hot dance of summer,
tarantellas and polkas under spiraling arms
of the Milky Way, hidden in rain
when I find a pretext to leave
early in the afternoon —
and my mother shuts the door.

MARTHE'S ALMANAC

Propped in bed, through years
of secret ills, Marthe reads histories
of Jeanne D'Albret, daughter
of Marguerite de Navarre,
La Reine Margot,
her court life memoirs of Gascony.

Zone time, apparent time, civil time,
it is wind through sand,
it is lamp black soot,
from the chimney flue.
She broods, riffling through chronicles
of what has run its course
along the river and past her house,
and though that woman, my mother, may stare
at the courtyard below, she will not see

women breaking flax for linen,
selling bread and silver,
spinning, carding, weaving,
hoisting sacks of wheat to the mill,
shelling peas, feeding geese.
None will draw vinegar and water from a keg,
shovel ashes, churn butter, brew ale,
nor stew small birds in iron kettles.

Marthe gazes out the window in August thunder,
September harvest, and each stroke of the hour
falls on her skin, on the slender watch
circling her wrist. What time is it?
Sometimes she forgets
what her serving girl says.
I am not there to hold a cup
of water to her lips, to comb her white hair.

Illuminated gold from the sun
writes elaborate initials on the water
and autumn clouds rise over the bridge.
I almost see her framed in a book of hours;
she is the woman skilled in calligraphy.
Winter scrolls gray light into a room
that holds her half asleep
as she lets a book fall to the floor,
loses count of the page.

WRITING LETTERS TO MY MOTHER

I sat inside a thin gray envelope of air
which seeped into my nerves, directing my hand
to write a stilted prose: how late I am
in sending condolences on the passing
of your sister, Jeanne, or the cool of spring
is followed by an excess of summer heat.

Looking up *abide* in the Thesaurus, I stared
at the "a" and "e", book ends to the word,
and the "b" and "d", twin sisters, one pregnant,
the other, an invalid in a wheelchair.
The central "i" kept the meaning intact. Abide,
endure, wait, reside, continue, tolerate,

bear with. To bear a child, to endure bearing it,
to let it reside in the womb, to wait for it
to come to term, to continue a time on earth,
tolerant of loss. An excess of summer heat
when I was born. She could not abide it. I endure.

What was the word to describe her only
sister strapped to a wheelchair in a ward?
What words must I pluck from a box of nouns
to suggest my mother's weltanschauung when she packed
me off to the nuns? Pain. Anger. Regret.
What are their referents?

There were days I pictured her
as a spectral ship that carried me, her cargo,
across the border from Paris to Brussels,
from autumn to summer, and to term.
Now she is dry docked in the country of her birth,
having voyaged through worlds of separate notions
and concerns from my beckoning messages.

I've changed my starts and paragraphs,
faltered and paused. How to capture a sentence?
What flourish to give it, how to end
on a roll, a firm note? Verbal *cul de sacs.*
I've dug them with my words to her.
Sometimes, my pen hovered over the page

like a dragonfly looking for a place
to land. This blue marsh of language,
this fen, that pure plateau at the head of the page,
the little strips between words and paragraphs
stretching out in parallel lines, or grid lines on a map.
My letters must have sighed between her forefinger and thumb.

Did she flinch at the curving scrawl that called
up the past she longed to dismiss like an unruly
class at the end of the day?
Composing the first draft of an answer, she turned
to the psalms, lifted her eyes to hills of white clouds —
heard God, her referent, calling her home.

HANDS

I watch the postman's
knobby hands bearing my letter.
Afraid someone might suspect something

out of the way, you tear it in two.
You fling it in the river.
Full of longing, my phrases, like my hands,

keep their distance from your fear.
Yet, old woman who never said my name,
I say if I could drop down beside you,

I would cover your hands in mine.
I would pull out the combs
to let your hair fall like a cloak,

all in a rush.
I would touch your lashes with my fingertips —
not in the house of your dry eyed gaze,

not in the room of your pinched lips
marking out words, so many
for your river's history, the local ruins

I might note in my wanderings —
but above the small door you form with your hands.
You, who once took my hand lightly in yours

but let it slip away.
You, reading the hours in shadows on the lawn,
the sweep hand of your watch will not have run

its term when your eyes curl back...
then my fingers will throb like birds
carrying strands of your hair to twine in their nests.

DAY VISITOR, SUSQUEHANNA UNIVERSITY

Sitting in a wingtip chair in a house of books,
canopy beds, hand sewn quilts, walls hung
with watercolor prints of the Susquehanna River,
I catch a whiff of ghosts, neurasthenic sisters
muttering stories behind latched doors.
Footfalls echoing on parquet...so many secrets
I cannot know cling like choked leaves to a garden
where a robin claims his ground with song.

What do birds sing in a Pyrenean spring?
Among stones in Espiens my mother
won't wake from a dream of running faster
than her elder sister over the stone bridge into town.
She won't gaze up at the watercolor print
of a barge on the Garonne. Others will disturb
her iron bed with sleep or love.

And the hand knit mauve and tea colored afghans,
the star patterned quilts will fold and unfold
without the shifts of her light boned body —
once it bore down that I might genuflect and sing,
released to troupes of robins on orphanage grounds,
to roses and ivy pruned by the Sisters,
reluctant mothers in an austere realm.

I hear footfalls of their brogans thud down
bare corridors, these strangers who would sometimes
pluck me from the river of crying mouths
to soothe me in a narrow bed where my story begins.

MY MOTHER'S COUNSELS

My mother said sleep in a bed of nettles
for suffering is natural.
And I've slept with burnt flowers, rust tipped
sunlight on my shears and trowels.
I've slept like a rake, cold teeth
pointed to the stars.
But never under her hand knit afghans,
my head on her pillowy breast, lips
parted and crusted with milk.
What if a rogue star came barrelling out of the sky
and He Whom You Know did not prevail? What then?
My mother said sew patches where the cloth is thin.
Salvation rewards the prepared.
I've sewn together the drunken
sun pounding outside my mother's door
with my thirst for a cup of water.
How calm her notion of God, an aha. An ah.
I was unprepared for her beauty
at eighty-five, tawny cheeks, a knob of hair
white as the tureen from which she spooned
boiled peas intently as a child.
What if all the towns burned down
under a giant asteroid? What of you and me?
She said His mystery is visible
then gazed beyond my nervous face
at stubbled fields,
at vast shuddering clouds.

A FAIRY TALE COUNTRY OF PALACES

She was like a forest where birds
came to brood. I likened them to gold-brown
leaves, to her eyes in November
when she buried the lover who fathered me.

Soon it was clear I favored him,
concupiscent lips, recalcitrant chin.
To blot him out from memory,
my mother dispatched me north of her hills.

Years later her crown of thin,
white hair glowed like a snowy pasture.
When she started to disappear, I began to compare
the amber in my eyes and my temple vein to hers.

Her narrow shoulders curved into light
resembled mine.
Photographed on her veranda, I saw myself
fingering her manuscript:

"Marguerite of Navarre; the Court at Nérac."
Beyond the river, hills crowned
the pastures with russet peaks.
For now that my mother turns

under the gold
rises of her countryside,
I am pulled towards her.
In a dream of an arbor I must pass through,

she grants me supple words, she coaxes,
my daughter, she says, my lost child.

REVERIES WHILE LANDING ON THE COAST

Blind swimmer at Mass, I believed
god lived in my mouth, in its membranes
and breath, uvula and roof, in everything
that bit into the foods of my communion.
I remember sweet wine but not my father's scent
of incense and fresh linen,
not his surplice and gown caught in the light,
white as the wafer pressed to his tongue,
polished and buffed as the moon of his nails,
when he heard confession or promoted the faith
in towns called after angels and saints.

In the sacristy, his parish on the coast,
he might have supposed a mammoth wave gathering
from a rift, dragging crosses and candles
out to drown, acts of contrition
bobbing in the tide like celebrants at Mass.
Where have the words of his ordination flown
and those of the last rites?
On the far side of a continent my father
has buried his holy orders, the account
of his broken vows. His notes on the seven
sacraments have crumbled like the carcasses of moths.

Western reaches. Over the hedgerows my childhood
skips off with a stick and a hoop, repeated novenas
and a crucifix. The past doesn't fit me.
I look back to see a priest and a lamb
in a dream of a daughter putting aside regret
and floating, as I do now
past lights blue as the auras
of believers who set out for heights
beyond the questions that rise and kneel
in long aisles of years, beyond the path
to the church doors bolted shut.

My Father in the West

Before he was ordained, where did he stand?
In what quadrant of the earth? If I could bring him down
like a slant of rain, a swift in flight.
To have heard the tumult of his heart against my hand.

My father and spiraea, coiled towards a mesmerizing blue. Grand
Teton wilds. My father and Woodland Star.
A heavy chested man, he bends to examine its basal leaves.
I cannot be there with my star charts to show him

the fleur-de-lis figure of Perseus, or Andromeda's blur
like milkweed dust. Mandates from Rome dissolve.
My father and wild strawberry, serrated,
heart shaped leaves. Bitterroot at summer's end

when he praised her lips, pink as clover
in an alpine meadow.
I will be their flower found in rimrock.
O My Father and arnica whose leaves disinfect wounds.

Yellow bells' flattened bulbs in the sagebrush bloom
after his body transmutes where I kneel,
astounded never to have gathered flowers for him,
nor blessed the seed, the mutiny of his fleshy root.

MY FATHER IN A GARDEN

In a photo of a garden at the century's
turn, you stand in front of Our Lady
of Sorrow, a heavy footed, bulldog
of a man, your head humming with orisons
and Latin verbs. Next to you
hydrangeas bend the boughs of the shrub,
blue as Mary's robe, as the dust your cassock
has become in a garden of stone
where the sea anoints the coast.

Bridegroom of Christ, writer of tracts,
my mother's lover, you never called me
daughter. I never called you father,
and after decades of Hail Mary ending in Gloria,
I come to this western garden not to look
at flowers but to ask, what am I to make
of these facts of you, you who will never trace
my eyebrows or my mouth.

They have blown away, these ardors
of another life when you were young,
your body stout in its priestly dark,
but not my words scattered on your grave
or the moment I invent: you snap off
your collar and turn, an ordinary father,
to embrace me in the garden.

MY PRIEST FATHER'S WORDS

Your words, my father, are clouds,
spirits to inhabit, things
to trace in the changes of light.

Where fish dart in the shallows
and the sun follows on the rise
of the island, in the circle

of birds, your *Historia Scholastica*
will vanish like these clouds, each

a life with its own shadow
on the earth as in your name
for me, uncalled for daughter,

as in my name for you,
father, Father.

MY FATHER AND THE LORD OF NULL

I seek my father, the Holy Bear in his surplice and gown. I find him prostrate on frozen stones. Skua gulls pray in a high mewling voice. To whom do they pray? The White Fox God, the Lord of Null, his blinding force. The penalty for silence is loss. I lose my father to the wind. Silence has everything to say and holds its breath. I will find the fish of miracles if someone tells how I came to be born in red moonlight, the eider duck's breast pressed to her eggs under the sign of the crab.

Dream Shore

I carry a ghost fish in a cage.
It has drifted from that other side
our dead slip through to look at us
with pleading eyes.
They ask what is this sleep
that takes place when we wake?
I say take wakening on faith,
and why have you come —
are the fathers here,
drowned friends,
my mother and her kin
from a Gascon rivertown?
I tell them ghosts go with us
when we dream, that each night
we fill a new dark
with fresh words,
glances not shared before.
They tell me their dreams
were fireflies at the river's
bend and vanished like sunlight
in the mouth of the fish,
in the shadow of the fisherman.

CLEMENCY

In front of a rooming house
she asks will I let her take my arm?
Her eyes aren't good. She tells me her father
who called her angel, my wren, is ashes.
The one who pressed roses into a book of verse,
mother, is a name smudged on stone.

Saved and never used, a trousseau:
camisoles and pillow lace, white satin shoes.
Like my mother, who looked the other way
when I was born, I want to escape
but the woman is intent on going somewhere
not far off with me in tow.

I imagine she lays the silver
for one, just like my solitary mother,
who did not confide in anyone.
We arrive. The woman tugs at my sleeve:
"Here stood my house."
Her hand waves towards an empty parking lot.

Eyes milky with cataracts, she tells her story:
"We wore tulle gowns for Mattie Clay's ball.
Father said 'Delia, Penelope, stop dillydallying.'
We had fire in the hearth. Servants below
readied for bed. Father consulted his watch,
said 'My duchesses are always late.

Go on without me. I've work to do.'
He struck a match to light his pipe.
We left by cab. Later his smile would disappear
along with my childhood in a blaze horses and water
could not put out."
Now with hours to burn in a town whose indolence

I will shrug off like a shawl in a overheated room,
I recollect my resolute mother who said go on
without me. The past grows cold.
I clasp another woman's hand in mine
as if she were my child.

Valéry Joins Me and My Newfound Cousin In Nérac

Maurice supposes she was fifteen when she sat
for the photographer, her second year at the lycée,
before she was caught off-guard
by me in her womb,

before she surrendered her claim
to fuss with my bib and teething ring.
Her photo shows smooth hair
pulled back into a bow.

Reverie: I see her browse
through Valéry's *Poèmes*,
half-parted lips — what do they say?
I tap her shoulder. She turns away, pauses,

allows the poet's words to brush her drowsy lids:
"Neither seen nor known, I am the perfume
living and dead come on the wind."
No use to tell her I also write poems.

In the shudder of dust on her piano,
"Für Elise" fades with "Traumerei" in a turn
of swiftly changing clouds over the river.
My mother, tender in a ribbed wool dress,

square wood buttons at the pockets.
I kiss the side part of her hair,
the wayward strand above her ear
and that shadow cast by the family nose,

long and thin like her face
framed in tooled leather.
In my poems she circles towards me
and away. In my poems she yields

under the weight of her lover and counts
cracks in the plaster. Where does she spin
her quandaries? Valéry waltzes her under the earth,
dizzy with the flesh of trees.

In My Cousin's Apartment, Paris 1994, Two Years After My Mother's Death

A cup that says *Bonjour*
returns my face as the child who saw
her first mirror
at the bottom of a bowl. Looped curls, lips,
eyes. Then my toys were sticks, woven grass.

I counted cracks in the floor, steps to Mass
and back. Clouds. Here they press their bellies
against a winter afternoon
in rooms where Mama smoothed her hair —
mirrors on every wall.

How many rosaries we murmured,
I, in the lowlands, Mama in France.
"Mary, Queen of Heaven, Blessed Art Thou."
These words crossed fields caked in snow,
mud, rain. Eating bread with jam

in mauve-gray weather, I fill this cup
with the longing to jumble the facts
of the story. The child finds shelter
next to her mother.
Sacksful of whatnots surround them

in the family salon. On a velvet settee
near the hand-carved buffet
the daughter reassures:
"You will see me bloom —
a red lily in a nun's pale room."

THE WIG OF LILIANE
(4 rue Brochant)

Chestnut colored, it droops
like a tender animal curled
in a bottom drawer
of the foyer chiffonnier.

My cousin Maurice, retired
professor of Latin and Greek,
keeps everything she wore:
hats, coats, purses, furs.

In every packed room her photograph —
wide apart eyes, level gray gaze,
neck length hair later shaved,
the offending lump plucked from her brain.

In the wig, snug under a slouched hat,
she revives to rummage for books
in dusty stores, striking a bargain
with dealers.

A hard to find translation
for Maurice cheers her, defers
the nausea, headaches he soothes
with a cloth dipped in cologne.

In this near museum of bric-a-brac,
posed in a dark Parisian spring,
Maurice confides in me.
A finch perched on her funeral wreath and sang.

After the burial, a pigeon
from the Parc Batignolle stood guard
on his shoulder. And inside the kitchen,
having misread the light of an open window,

a sparrow circled her needlepoint
of birds and sky. We hear a stir
at the door. Flinging the wig to the floor,
she floats into the vestibule, breathless

with the purchase of Martial's *Epigrams*.
A scarce edition, leather bound, deep brown
like her damp hair, whose true shade
matches the hue of the antique buffet

looming in the mirrored hall.
The bird roosts in her outstretched palm.
As soon as she nudges it back on course,
she will cradle my face in her hands,

examine me as if I were another rare book
she'd stumbled on at the *bouquiniste*.
"Maurice, *chéri*, look, our cousin has something
of her mother's eyes about the lids, the lift

of the brow, but Aunt Jeanne's hair,
the flyaway curls."

A PLACE AT THE TABLE

"Today I climbed the Jungfrau. Incomparable.
Love, J." She will write about the war,
her Legion of Honor, Kuala Lumpur, Cairo, Kabul.

At the last, Aunt Jeanne is tethered
to a wheelchair
in the same room where my mother wrote me,
"No one must know you exist."

I met Jeanne once in Paris.
She handed me a snapshot of her sister in a hat
like a helmet pressed to the face of a saint.
"We don't get on," she shrugged.

Years later cousin Maurice dusts off a photo of Jeanne
posed in jodhpurs and boots, blouse flared open
at the neck. The sky is brushed by blowzy clouds,
her look says she longs for the summit.

I superimpose a photo of myself
as a girl leaning back on a rock,
my face to the sun. But I could be a seedling
blown from an alpine meadow,

a minus sign on a layer of stone.
In this shot the family takes supper by the river.
Posed alongside an empty chair, Jeanne leans
towards my grandparents,

regal Marie and silvery Alfred.
An ambiguous smile playing at her lips,
my mother stands apart.
When I enter that frame, I collect a skim

of imagined kisses. Questions dart
like damsel flies: The school year?
Holiday plans? And will I climb the Pyrenees with Jeanne?

GASCON VOICES

Not far from Espiens
Matthieu Dulong asked her to dance
at the Feast of Saint Anne.
On All Souls Day, picking chanterelles at dusk,

her path grew confused
and wolves rushed in packs, eyes like white coals.
"Elizabeth!" She swerved to see Matthieu
pointing his rifle. So in a dream of Gascony,

my great-grandmother speaks to me
in the foothills of the Pyrenees.
I see a flash; her dark blue dress,
white fichu and silver brooch.

Syllables blur as she rushes her story.
In Gascony I wake to the scent
of tea roses swollen with rain, to linen sheets,
a swirled blue "D" embroidered at the hem.

Strands of loosened hair or a web?
A flutter as a hand brushes my ear.
She whispers, "On this day of Saint Denise,
come to the churchyard,

your mother is there" — my shadowy mother
who guarded the secrets
I release like caged birds —
"and one can see the Pyrenees."

In a piping voice Elizabeth coaxes, but I pull away
into morning's bees in the blue salvia,
rust colored tiles, the buzz of the river
and an inclination to linger

another quarter of an hour, an immigrant
between waking and dreams of women murmuring their names
under rain soaked stones
in Espiens, cradle of my origins.

III

THINGS DREAM OF THEIR LIKENESSES AND NEEDS

One summer I dreamed bees brushed
my legs with their fur, a buzzing
alarm fled from the shrub. Talk
rose and fell like knees at High
Mass and bees disappeared
in a thin trail of dust, a comet
gobbled by the sun.

What do things which vanish dream?
Ghost butterflies, rabbits, invisible
ink scrawling a story where padlocks
dream of keys, hinges of doors, and
above the crenelated roofs: quarks
and atomic particles. Not much is known
of their likenesses and needs.

Snow coming down is not stars. Quark
dust may dream of the dark pouring out
its galaxies. On our little ball, women
haul water and men stir hives. Little
is known, they say at night drinking honeyed
wine, quoting homilies: desire comes
before love, the wife of a hunter
may not spin while he eats.

Desire devours my days. I change positions
in a bed which dreams intersecting points
and nodes. In my land and water dreams, lakes
eat stones, trees eat birds. Leaves give their names
when they fall. The bare branch takes
snow for nourishment.

Great books say nothing suffers death.
Spring: lark and bluet. The cuckoo
abandons her eggs in an unfamiliar nest.
I guard my secret names. Little is known
of the summer to come, disordered sleep
in off-kilter days, the reckoning of dreams.

THE PERSEID METEORS OF AUGUST

Only insect insomniacs turn up the volume
of their music, oblivious
to the celestial visitors whose paths
arrive and depart for us.

We, who crane our necks upward,
wait for them to speed past the meadow's
silverrod, candelabras of vervain,
past that *garrup* of the bullfrog in the pond
as he calls for his share of rapture.

One then another, they hurtle over the barn
beyond farm lights and outlying reaches of town.
Tipped into earth they jostle the dreams
of our ancestors

and the about-to-be-born who are crowning.
Blood smeared, out of their mothers's pods
they hammer the air with cries
to the heaven overhead that does not see them.

August Atoms

Daubed blurs. In the meadow
the painter brushes lead white
sunlit clouds on cloth,
and the sculptor perched on a rock

quarters an apple.
Hunched over a text,
I say it is calligraphy to bees,
that grasshoppers have spotted

syntactical errors.
Insect galaxies signal
from their splotch of grass
where cinquefoil shimmers like butter.

And the chipmunk skittering away
from the cat
curls in a pure knot
of opalescent light

like the flicker,
a fuzz of worm dazed in its beak.
Cone headed katydid, carpenter ant,
ourselves born to gather meaning

like ravenous bees in the goldenrod,
all bobble through waves we cannot see
wash over us in a buzzing calm
or discombobulation of the field.

MAUNDERINGS AT LAMMASTIDE

Born to the botanist,
I would have swept cuttings
of ranunculus into the bin.
Begot to the biologist,
probed mitochondria.

I brush away cutworm moths,
riddled leaves, wait for Perseid
meteors to give value to their origins.
Dust of my sires clouds the road.
Prelate's child, I pull a wagon of misgivings

and renounce the wafer taken from the paten.
Archivist's child, I muddle recollections
in my hive of facts, tilt a Celestron-8
towards the Dipper called The Wagon
by Druid ministers of stars.

HARD MUSE

"Too many embellishments —
dump that pallid wash of blue
at some one else's door.
Verbal murk pollutes your work.
Abandon jonquils, pale rain,

dew on trillium. You're like a lover
who's exhausted every posture,"
she says, peering over my shoulder.
"Too much cascade, ripple and froth.
Get rid of the bromide of love

budding into song under a wan sky.
Things frilled or blurred in fog,
fringed, lobed, starred, only go
so far. Better have juncoes flying
in a silver ring, bloodroot

and toothwort in the woods.
You've too many twittery, ashen,
flesh pink Boucher cherub phrases,
pearl sheen dawn and bluet praises.
'To conjugate a woodpecker's tap tap

as it probes for grub above the lap
of water on mossy shrub,'
smacks of the ornate.
Tu Fu said ideas in poems
should be simple and noble.

Think of words as radishes, biting and sharp,
planted in a well drained patch.
Go back and revise," she gives me a stern look,
slashing my grade in her record book.

Moth Dream of My Late Therapist

You stand in a dim room
pinching a moth
between forefinger and thumb.
The lines around your lips,
the notes on your pad are spidery,

an old man's shaky penmanship.
I say my life has taken a positive turn
like the hands of a watch
in a revelatory hour.
I say I was prepared to give my son

your name but nothing dropped from my womb.
Had it, the child would be long past
studying wing prints in a microscope.
He will never tug at your arm
for the butterfly book you carried

to the vineyard. I remember swarms of leaves
and stars like birds staggered overhead
when I wanted to use my head
as a gavel on your desk. It held
a paperweight. Was it a fruit fly

trapped in glass? You ask, "The moth?
What comes to mind?" My son's name
banging its wings at the door of the dream,
the pallor of the clock when I silence the alarm.

IN PRAISE OF OUTLINES

In Illinois, a state edging
the five Great Lakes that open
like petals of a flower on the map,
I see America: straightbacked bull
on the northern frontier, hindquarters in the west.
The penis in New Orleans inseminates the Gulf
and one legged Florida kicks up shrimp
where Cuba casts nets of phosphorescent scales.

And where Costa Rica's calf
squeezes into Panama's boot
I step into South America,
a cone set afloat in the sea,
rippled by winds
that play the Andes like a xylophone.
Look, that fire in the llama's eye
is brushed by the light of Volans and Crux.

Antarctica. In the mirage of Queen Maude's Land
buried in snow and explorers' routes,
I imagine I chase ghost clouds, the breath
of Amundsen, Scott and Byrd,
count horizon lines lost, time numbed in the cold.

Orchids and torpor. I muse on empires
of jade in Thailand and Vietnam. On the map
these countries are a monkey's head
sniffing the Gulf of Siam. Australia's horn
gores the Torres Straits,
Tasmania's shield is cast adrift to float
in a Tasman Sea whose shipping lines
I pretend to sail.

Dazed from invented journeys,
I close the pages of a gazetteer
in a kitchen with windows that look out
on a spray of stars in The Milky Way, advancing
from north to south like two peninsulas,
like coral reefs.

Encounter at the Jardins Botaniques

This boy who looks like my husband
combs his spiked hair with long fingers.
He might be my son, an immigrant
from a memory I can't place or name.
Intricate station, the day
announces clouds that arrive

and take leave over domes of the city.
The voice is gruff when he commands:
give me your rosary.
I stare at his lilac tinted sleepy lids.
Even his hips, set low
on a long waisted frame

resemble my husband's.
When I cajole, "I'll stitch your name
to the back of your shirt,
I'll butter your green
and yellow vegetables,
buy you toy trains and holy figurines,"

he runs past tulip poplars
and maidenhair fern.
In a honey colored blotch of rain,
there goes my son:
Jean-Luc, Michel, Marcel, Alain?

IN A GARDEN
for Abea

We sidestep ferns and shrubs, I
with scrawls for a poem, you
with Wei-li, her straight shouldered
walk mimicking yours.
I remember your blue embroidered blouse
with butterfly sleeves
that caught the wind when you ran,
your banner of black hair.
Was it ten years ago?
Before Wei-li was given her name
meaning "grand beauty" in Mandarin,
before you visited Beijing
and sent me a red scarf printed
with Chinese characters. What did they say?
Something Confucian about family decorum?
I wondered if heaven had spoken to your kin
as to our fathers, the reverends.
In this same garden we talked
of the children we might bring to term,
of our mothers past longing.
Now the boundaries of trees grow blurred.
Pushing back insect riddled leaves,
we find a path out of the nettles that sting
our legs. I, past child bearing,
watch Wei-li as she tames her hair
with comb and barrette, and wait
for a Red Admiral butterfly,
listless in August's late afternoon,
to arrive and depart. Across the water
in a garden of stone my mother learns repose.
A breeze combs the yellow grass. I fold away
my words. Nothing has devoured the knobbed moon
that rises white as sweet elysium
whose odor of honey rouses bees.

Teaching Junior High at Castle Hill

I did not. You did.
Lester and carrot top Max dust the floor
with their fisticuffs. Large Marjorie weeps
into my handkerchief. Max likes you, I say.
That jerk, she wipes her nose, sashays
from the room, an odor of spray in her rippled hair.
Select the word you think fits most.

My curled down lips announce the Pledge.
Dust traps the light, chalk on my sleeves.
In a snow of quizzes, papers swirl.
Splintered blades of ceiling fans spin
lesson plans and calendars.
Move from simple to complex.

A spider races up my face, fits the contours of its web
over my recall, half dreaming on that line
to Castle Hill, sleeping parts of speech
about to wake in my leather case
when the school bell chimed. True or false?
Contrast. Compare.

CONFOUNDED SONG

Amber in autumn, the orchards —
bob-dog rampages between trees

silver in winter the hunter
brushes pines with his quiver

of arrows and dog slavers
at Hare in the Sky

wants to haul it by the throat
but so much fire confounds him

and Dog Star blinds his path — are those bear
tracks in snow? — he dreams

the hunter calls from the orchard:
wake, bone white clouds in a blue

dog dish, look, birch bark,
spring stars and summer's scorpion pokes

at the seam between heaven and earth,
"Goodboy, run."

CONSOLATION OF BLOOD AND IRISES

In the glass some arrangement of Inez
in her life zone breathes a cloudlet of mist.

She has a chance to shake off the weather
of her past like a tiger in the rain.

Her veins obey the written course.
Nothing derelict in what blood knows

repeating its feat of memory. Few consolations
arrive without words. Striped irises

in an orange vase allow the dark to blunder in
and be comforted. Whispered through blinds or fronds,

the Tupi word for mirror and water is the same,
both sink roots of rippled light.

Such reflections save Inez and her
like-minded kin from the beast of the invisible.

FIRE IN THE PRAIRIE

hisses
in the wind
as I begin to blur
hours I learned
to scrawl
oak, elm, pine, palm
in cursives at school
rehearsed with the teacher
in powder blue
or rose, her pompadour
or coronet of braids —
I forget where
she touched
my wrist lightly as a leaf
and I smelled oil
of cloves
and wintergreen
on her handkerchief.
Clouds of chalk dust
speed back in time.
A school of leaves
lets out the cold,
birds stop
darting from shrub
to grove
in that storm
when my mother and father
kicked off their shoes
and bits and speckles
that would be me
pleaded to be born
in a cocoon.
Fire in the pepper grass
soon put out.
Charred roots rise.
Ghost-snow calls.

TRANSFORMATIONS

Say we are Monarchs
migrating by day to Sonoran hills.
A lepidopterist will catch us
through binoculars and nod.
He has seen our kind
convening in clouds.
Summer perturbations on the wings
of a Snout, Admiral, Viceroy, White.

Say one, two, a thousand years
are milkweed floss set loose.
What then? The two of us,
ghost butterflies, have frittered away
our lives again. The lepidopterist
snaps us in his net. He has seen our sort
before. Knobs, bumps, hairs, horns,
weren't we caterpillars once?

We watch him spear grubs
to roast in a fire. Wing shaped flames,
rising ash migrates from jungle
to the flutter of stars. Say the last
of this world will fly on the back
of a Metalmark, that Reakert's Blues
are marshaled in the field. What then?
We will hide in a damp cocoon and start again.

CARNEGIE MELLON POETRY

1975
The Living and the Dead, Ann Hayes
In the Face of Descent, T. Alan Broughton

1976
The Week the Dirigible Came, Jay Meek
Full of Lust and Good Usage, Stephen Dunn

1977
How I Escaped from the Labyrinth and Other Poems, Philip Dacey
The Lady from the Dark Green Hills, Jim Hall
For Luck: Poems 1962-1977, H.L. Van Brunt
By the Wreckmaster's Cottage, Paula Rankin

1978
New & Selected Poems, James Bertolino
The Sun Fetcher, Michael Dennis Browne
A Circus of Needs, Stephen Dunn
The Crowd Inside, Elizabeth Libbey

1979
Paying Back the Sea, Philip Dow
Swimmer in the Rain, Robert Wallace
Far from Home, T. Alan Broughton
The Room Where Summer Ends, Peter Cooley
No Ordinary World, Mekeel McBride

1980
And the Man Who Was Traveling Never Got Home, H.L. Van Brunt
Drawing on the Walls, Jay Meek
The Yellow House on the Corner, Rita Dove
The 8-Step Grapevine, Dara Wier
The Mating Reflex, Jim Hall

1981
A Little Faith, John Skoyles
Augers, Paula Rankin
Walking Home from the Icehouse, Vern Rutsala
Work and Love, Stephen Dunn
The Rote Walker, Mark Jarman
Morocco Journal, Richard Harteis
Songs of a Returning Soul, Elizabeth Libbey

1982
The Granary, Kim R. Stafford
Calling the Dead, C.G. Hanzlicek
Dreams Before Sleep, T. Alan Broughton
Sorting It Out, Anne S. Perlman
Love Is Not a Consolation; It Is a Light, Primus St. John

1983
The Going Under of the Evening Land, Mekeel McBride
Museum, Rita Dove
Air and Salt, Eve Shelnutt
Nightseasons, Peter Cooley

1984
Falling from Stardom, Jonathan Holden
Miracle Mile, Ed Ochester
Girlfriends and Wives, Robert Wallace
Earthly Purposes, Jay Meek
Not Dancing, Stephen Dunn
The Man in the Middle, Gregory Djanikian
A Heart Out of This World, David James
All You Have in Common, Dara Wier

1985
Smoke from the Fires, Michael Dennis Browne
Full of Lust and Good Usage, Stephen Dunn *(2nd edition)*
Far and Away, Mark Jarman
Anniversary of the Air, Michael Waters
To the House Ghost, Paula Rankin
Midwinter Transport, Anne Bromley

1986
Seals in the Inner Harbor, Brendan Galvin
Thomas and Beulah, Rita Dove
Further Adventures With You, C.D. Wright
Fifteen to Infinity, Ruth Fainlight
False Statements, Jim Hall
When There Are No Secrets, C.G. Hanzlicek

1987
Some Gangster Pain, Gillian Conoley
Other Children, Lawrence Raab
Internal Geography, Richard Harteis
The Van Gogh Notebook, Peter Cooley
A Circus of Needs, Stephen Dunn (2nd edition)
Ruined Cities, Vern Rutsala
Places and Stories, Kim R. Stafford

1994
If Winter Come: Collected Poems, 1967–1992, Alvin Aubert
Of Desire and Disorder, Wayne Dodd
Ungodliness, Leslie Adrienne Miller
Rain, Henry Carlile
Windows, Jay Meek
A Handful of Bees, Dzvinia Orlowsky

1995
Germany, Caroline Finkelstein
Housekeeping in a Dream, Laura Kasischke
About Distance, Gregory Djanikian
Wind of the White Dresses, Mekeel McBride
Above the Tree Line, Kathy Mangan
In the Country of Elegies, T. Alan Broughton
Scenes from the Light Years, Anne C. Bromley
Quartet, Angela Ball

1996
Back Roads, Patricia Henley
Dyer's Thistle, Peter Balakian
Beckon, Gillian Conoley
The Parable of Fire, James Reiss
Cold Pluto, Mary Ruefle
Orders of Affection, Arthur Smith
Colander, Michael McFee

1997
Growing Darkness, Growing Light, Jean Valentine
Selected Poems, 1965-1995, Michael Dennis Browne
Your Rightful Childhood: New and Selected Poems, Paula Rankin
Headlands: New and Selected Poems, Jay Meek
Soul Train, Allison Joseph
The Autobiography of a Jukebox, Cornelius Eady
The Patience of the Cloud Photographer, Elizabeth Holmes
Madly in Love, Aliki Barnstone
An Octave Above Thunder: New and Selected Poems, Carol Muske

1998
Yesterday Had a Man in It, Leslie Adrienne Miller
Definition of the Soul, John Skoyles
Dithyrambs, Richard Katrovas
Postal Routes, Elizabeth Kirschner
The Blue Salvages, Wayne Dodd
The Joy Addict, James Harms
Clemency, Colette Inez
Scattering the Ashes, Jeff Friedman
Sacred Conversations, Peter Cooley
Life Among the Trolls, Maura Stanton